Ancient Egypt
For Kids
Written by
Rich Linville

ISBN: 9781520629292

It is 50,000 BC during the Stone Age. I am wandering around with a group of hunter-gatherers. We use stones for tools. We are thirsty and hungry. What's that ahead of us?

It's a fresh water river. We call it "Nile" which means river and this place we call "Egypt" which means "rich river soil." There are plenty of fish and wild plants to eat.

Where in the world do you think Egypt is located?

The red circle is Mexico.
The yellow circle is Egypt.
The blue circle is India.

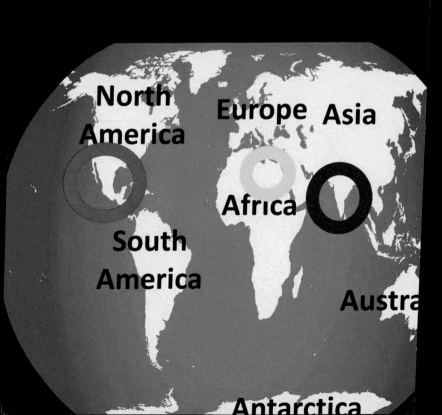

10,000 BC in Egypt, I am a hunter- gatherer. I use a stone tied to a wooden stick to spear fish in the river. I hunt turtles and dig up roots to eat. I dry reeds to make baskets to hold food.

Now it is 9,500 BC. I am an Egyptian farmer. I discover that I can plant wild wheat and barley to grow and harvest my own food. If I store the extra grains, I don't have to wander around looking for food.

The main food of both wealthy and poor Egyptians is bread and beer made from wheat and barley. Rarely do we have meat and vegetables. We use stones to grind grains to create flour to make bread. Our teeth are worn by the broken bits of stone that are in the flour and bread.

Around 5000 BC, I live in the Nile Valley with a small tribe. I make jewelry, combs, and bracelets from copper. I decorate small and large ceramic pots that hold food and water.

We trade with surrounding people for gold, ivory, natural obsidian glass and lapis which is a deep blue stone. We become a wealthy, dominant civilization with leaders who rule the people of the Nile Valley. The symbol for our leader is a falcon bird and a white crown.

About 3500 BC, we Egyptians draw rock pictures of everything around us. With about 1,000 drawings, we can write with pictures. It is called hieroglyphs (high-row-gliffs). We believe that the god Thoth who has the head of an ibis bird invented writing and gave it to us Egyptians.

Here is an example of Egyptian picture writing called hieroglyphs. Can you find the picture words for vulture bird, eye, eyes, and river? This writing was used by Egyptians for over 3,000 years until 400 AD.

For fun, if you want to write your name in Egyptian picture writing, draw or sketch the red symbol for each letter in your name.

A		H	
B		I	
C		J	
D		K	
E		L	
F		M	
G		N	
O		V	
P		W	
Q		Y	
R		Z	
S		CH	
T		KH	
U		SH	

Around 3100 BC, a change in the climate creates the Sahara Desert west of the Nile River. Before then, the Sahara had trees.

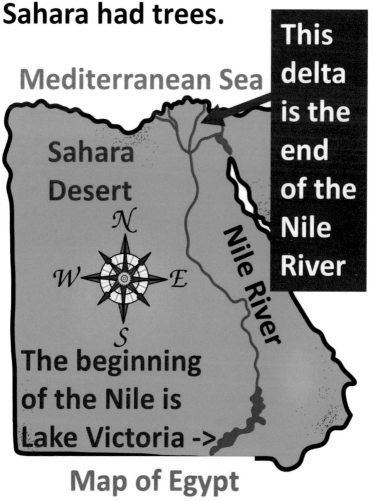

Mediterranean Sea

This delta is the end of the Nile River

Sahara Desert

N

W   E

S

Nile River

The beginning of the Nile is Lake Victoria ->

Map of Egypt

Not much is known about the early Egyptian pharaohs. Some writings say that Menes-Narmer (mee-neez nahr-mur) is the first pharaoh. He unites Upper (southern) and Lower (northern) Egypt around 3100 BC. It's written that he inherited the throne and crown of Egypt from the god Horus who has the head of a falcon bird.

King Menes-Narmer is said to have ruled Egypt for 60 years. He was given a sheepherder's whip and crook which may be symbolic of ruling the Egyptian people (whip) and helping them (a crook pulls a sheep out of danger).

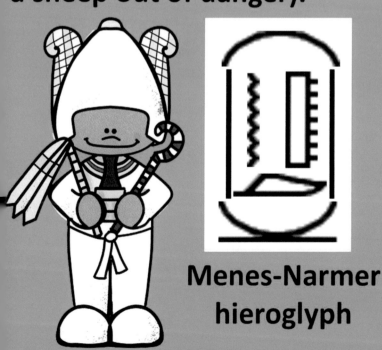

Menes-Narmer hieroglyph

Near the Nile marshes in 3000 BC, we picked and cut reed plants to make a paper called papyrus. Look! In the marsh eating a snail is an Ibis bird or is it the Egyptian god Thoth?

In one of three ways, we cut the three-side reed into strips. We lay the flat strips on top of each other crossing at right angles. We hit them with a stone to make a flat sheet of paper. The reeds have a natural glue to make the papyrus. The flat sheet of paper is rolled up and stored in boxes.

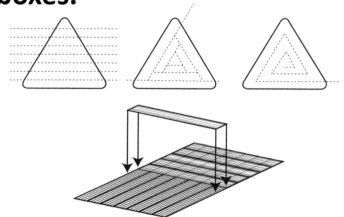

Unrolling the papyrus, we place stones on the edges to keep it open. The scribes or writers use a reed brush with ink made from water and powdered rocks to draw and write on the papyrus. Here is an ancient Egyptian book made from papyrus.

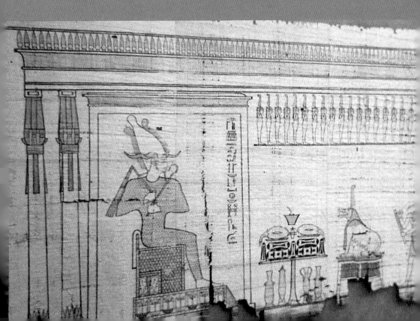

Around 2600 BC, this 6 step pyramid is built to be the burial tomb of the third dynasty (empire) Pharaoh Djoser (joe-sir). It is the first large structure to be made of a cut stone called limestone. It's higher than a 20 story building (200 feet or 60 meters).

From 2600 BC to 2100 BC with strong pharaohs, the farmers produce more and more food and the population of Egypt increases. This period of time is called the Old Kingdom. The vizier (viz-ee-ur) is the highest official that serves the king or pharaoh. He sends out tax collectors to collect a part of the Egyptian farmers' crops.

The vizier with the crops collected by taxing the farmers can now pay workers to specialize. So that water from the Nile can flood the land to grow more crops, the vizier pays workers to dig irrigation canals.

wheat field with an irrigation canal dug by paying workers

The vizier has a justice system to keep peace and order. When someone breaks a law, they are judged by the pharaoh or vizier. If found guilty, he may have his face cut up to show that he committed a crime. He may be fined (gold or grain) or be exiled from Egypt or else he may be beaten with a whip.

Also, the vizier pays around 10,000 workers at a time with bread and beer to build statues, buildings, monuments and pyramids for the pharaohs such as these 6 stone pyramids of Giza. It took about 30 years to build a pyramid.

About 2500 BC, the Great Pyramid of Giza (gee-zah) is also known as the Pyramid of Khufu (koo-foo) or Cheops (key-awps) is built. Nearby is the Sphinx (sfinks) with the body of a lion and the head of Khufu.

The 6 stone pyramids of Giza are built to bury the pharaoh deep inside with objects that the pharaoh would need for the next world after death. Egyptians who are not important are buried under small piles of stones. This keeps wild animals from digging up and mutilating the dead body before it goes to the next world.

As the population grew larger, there was a need for more officials to run the government and more scribes to keep records of laws and taxes collected.

Statue of a scribe who is cross-legged reading a tablet.

Temples are built to worship the Egyptian gods and to remember the pharaohs. The religious leaders and their followers are given land and gold by the pharaoh.

Along with droughts and famines, the pharaohs are challenged by the lesser rulers or governors. Because the pharaohs waste too much, they lose power and influence. This is called the First Intermediate Period.

During the Middle Kingdom (2134–1690 BC), Egypt begins to be prosperous again by conquering and farming more land. The military takes land that has gold mines and stone mines. A wall and bridges are built with water canals filled with crocodiles to protect against attacks.

Around 1700 BC from different places in Asia, the Hyksos (hick-sos) invade Egypt. With over-mining, too much waste and extreme flooding of the Nile River, Egypt declines into a Second Intermediate

These settlers from Asia bring fresh ideas to Egypt. The Hyksos bring new crops and animals as well as the horse and chariot. These new ideas will help the future Egypt.

From 1550 to 1069 BC, the pharaohs of the New Kingdom of Egypt extend their influence to become the largest empire ever. In 1507–1458 BC, a woman pharaoh, Hatshepsut (hat-shep-suit) expands the size of Egypt, restores trade with other places and promotes peace.

In 1333 BC, Pharaoh Tutankhamun (Too-tan-common) or King Tut becomes the ruler of Egypt when he is about ten years old. He has very good viziers and military leaders to help him rule.

Painted wooden statue of King Tut as a boy.

At the age of 19, King Tut dies. He is wrapped in linen cloth. A gold mask is placed over his head and he is placed in a coffin. He is buried in a tomb in the Valley of the Kings.

The wealth of the Egyptians leads to corruption in the government and also to invasions. The Libyans from the west and Assyrians from the northeast attack and weaken Egypt. It enters into the Third Intermediate Period which occurs from 1069 BC to 653 BC.

After 653 BC, Ancient Egypt becomes weaker when it loses battles to Babylonian kings and the Persians. Even though the once great empire of Ancient Egypt collapses, for the ordinary Egyptians very little changes in their daily lives of farming.

Achievements
of Ancient Egypt

Ancient Egyptians made many achievements:

1. Art
2. Writing
3. Medicine
4. Math
5. First known Peace Treaty
6. Cutting rocks for building
7. Measuring farm boundaries
8. Building pyramids and temples
9. Irrigation
10. Boat making with planks

Timeline of Ancient Egypt

Note: Historians do not all agree on these dates.

50,000 BC hunter-gatherers in Egypt

9,500 BC farming in Egypt

3,500 BC hieroglyphs

3,100 BC Sahara Desert formed

3,100 BC First Egyptian pharaoh Menes-Narmer

3,000 BC papyrus made

2,600 BC step pyramid and Pharaoh Djoser

2,500 BC Great Pyramid of Giza and Sphinx of Khufu

1,700 BC Hyksos invade Egypt

1,500 BC Queen Hatshepsut brings trade and peace to Egypt

1,333 BC King Tut

653 BC Ancient Egypt conquered by Babylonians

Ancient Egypt Periods

Note: Historians do not all agree on these dates.

50,000-3,150 BC
Prehistoric Egypt

3150–2686 BC
Early Dynastic Period

2686–2181 BC
Old Kingdom

2181–2055 BC
1st Intermediate Period

2055–1650 BC
Middle Kingdom

1650–1550 BC
2nd Intermediate Period

1550–1069 BC
New Kingdom

1069–664 BC
3rd Intermediate Period

664–332 BC
Late Period

Thank you for reading this book about Ancient Egypt. Written by Rich Linville and dedicated to my grandchildren Kai and Mia and everyone who is interested in Ancient Egypt. Illustrations from Commons Wiki, OpenClipArt, and purchased from Edu-Clips.

If you like unicorn jokes, you might enjoy:

Unicorn Jokes for Kids
Riddles with Pictures

You also might like to read:

Rocky the Hopping Penguin
Who Never Quits
By Rich Linville

Rocky goes on an adventure from the ocean to his island and back again. Sadly, the numbers of rockhopper penguins is on the decline. They may become extinct unless something is done about them.

Funny Sayings
for Kids
Book 1

What do you think these funny sayings mean?

Written by Rich Linville
with Pictures

Our Solar System with Space Riddles

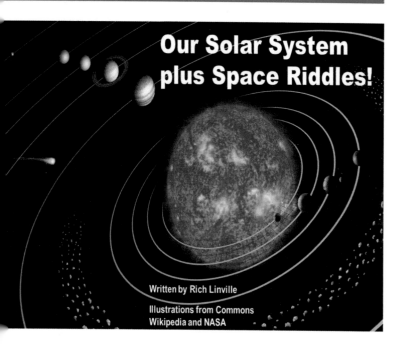

Our Solar System plus Space Riddles!

Written by Rich Linville

Illustrations from Commons Wikipedia and NASA

Actual photos of our sun, planets and a dwarf planet. Learn about our solar system with a trick to remember the order of the planets.

Made in the USA
Middletown, DE
09 September 2018